PICTURE LIBRARY

ICE SPORTS

PICTURE LIBRARY

ICE SPORTS

Norman Barrett

Franklin Watts

London   New York   Sydney   Toronto

© 1988 Franklin Watts Ltd

First published in Great Britain
    1988 by
Franklin Watts Ltd
12a Golden Square
London W1R 4BA

First published in the USA by
Franklin Watts Inc
387 Park Avenue South
New York
NY 10016

First published in Australia by
Franklin Watts
14 Mars Road
Lane Cove
NSW 2066

UK ISBN: 0 86313 684 2
US ISBN: 0-531-10627-6
Library of Congress Catalog Card
Number 88-50382

Printed in Italy

Designed by
Barrett & Willard

Photographs by
Action Plus
Eileen Langsley/Action Plus
N.S. Barrett Collection

Illustrations by
Rhoda & Robert Burns

Technical Consultant
Howard Bass

Contents

Introduction

Ice sports are enjoyed both indoors and out. Ice skating is practiced by young and old alike. It is a pleasant and exciting pastime, and at the most advanced level is a graceful and thrilling sport.

Ice hockey is a tough, skillful game, the fastest team sport in the world. Other ice sports include curling, in which players slide flat stones across the ice, and iceboating.

△ Figure skating is a graceful, athletic sport, performed solo or in pairs, as shown here. Each performance is marked by a panel of judges.

The two main ice skating sports are figure skating and speed skating.

In figure skating, competitors perform routines to music. Points are awarded by a panel of judges for both skill and artistry. There are separate events for men, women and mixed pairs, and for ice dancing.

In speed skating, competitors race in pairs around a two-lane oval track. The object is to clock the fastest time.

△ Goal! The puck – a small rubber disc – flashes into the net. Ice hockey is a rough, tough, fast-moving team sport.

Looking at ice sports

Figure skate
The blade of a figure skate has a set of saw-like teeth at the toe, called a toe-rake. This helps in spinning and in certain jumps. The underside of the blade is grooved, so that there are two edges. Most movements are performed on one of these edges.

Speed skate
A speed skate is longer than a figure skate and has a straight, flat, thinner blade. Its upper edge is reinforced with steel tubing. The boot, with low ankle supports, looks more like a shoe.

Ice hockey skate
An ice hockey skate is about half the thickness of a figure blade but is reinforced with hollow tubing. The ends of the blade are curved to help maneuvering, and a guard must be worn on the heel. The boot has reinforced heel and toe caps.

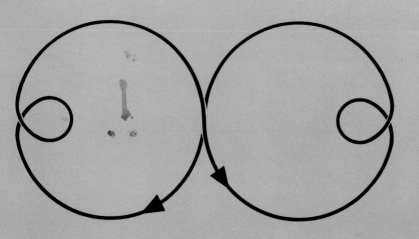

Cutting figures
In the compulsory part of figure skating, figures are traced in the ice. This one is called a paragraph-loop and is more difficult than it looks.

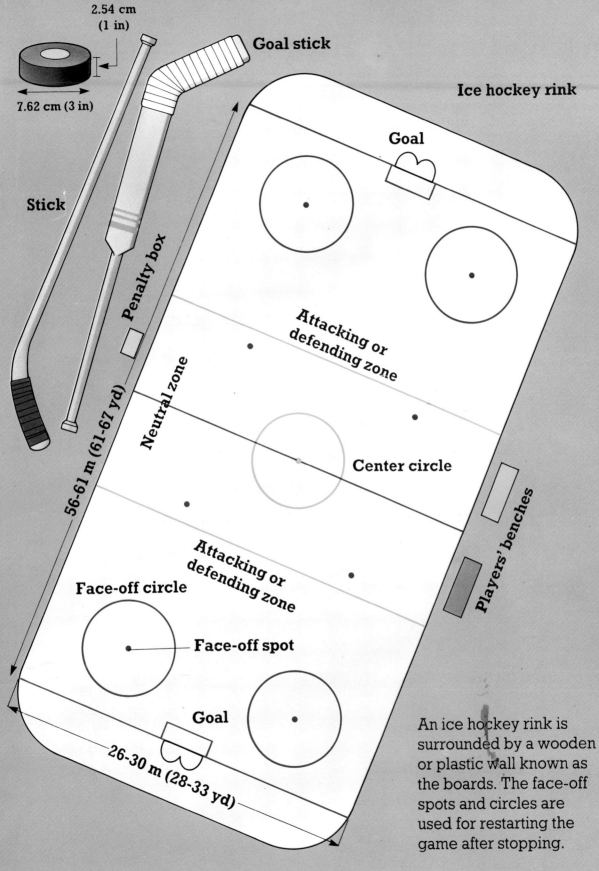

2.54 cm
(1 in)

7.62 cm (3 in)

Goal stick

Ice hockey rink

Stick

Goal

Penalty box

Attacking or
defending zone

Neutral zone

56-61 m (61-67 yd)

Center circle

Players' benches

Attacking or
defending zone

Face-off circle

Face-off spot

Goal

26-30 m (28-33 yd)

An ice hockey rink is
surrounded by a wooden
or plastic wall known as
the boards. The face-off
spots and circles are
used for restarting the
game after stopping.

9

Figure skating

In figure skating, there are three sections – compulsory figures, short program and free skating.

The compulsory figures account for 30 per cent of a skater's total score. There are a number of set figures that a skater has to trace, consisting of circles, loops and turns. The judges look for posture, balance and steady speed as well as a correctly traced figure.

△ Myriam Oberwiler of Switzerland performs a split jump during her Olympic free-skating program. The free skating is the most exciting and spectacular section of competitive ice skating. It makes up 50 per cent of the total points.

In the two-minute short program, worth 20 per cent of the total points, skaters perform the same seven moves. They choose their own music and the order of the moves, which include jumps and spins.

In the free-skating program – 5 minutes for men, 4 for women – the skaters perform their own routines to their own choice of music. Judges award marks for technical merit and for artistic impression.

▽ Concentration is etched on the faces of two great champions and rivals, Brian Orser of Canada (right) and Brian Boitano of the US. Jumps must be landed on the correct edge of the skate with pinpoint accuracy.

△ The grace and beauty of figure skating have led to its description as "ballet on ice." These lifts in pairs skating show why.

◁ Simone Koch of East Germany performing a catch-hold spin. Spins should be done on one spot without movement from that spot.

Pairs perform a 2¼-minute short program of set moves and a free-skating routine of 4½ minutes.

The partners combine to perform spins, lifts, and throws from jumps. They also do matching movements while separated, including jumps and spins.

For lifts and spirals especially, it helps if the male partner is strong and the female light. Marks are awarded like the solo events.

▷ US champions Gillian Wachsman and Todd Waggoner perform a death spiral, one of the most graceful and daring of all pair skating movements.

The man spins around on the spot while swinging his partner at full length. She circles around him, bent over backward and supported on one skate, getting lower and lower until her head almost brushes the ice.

Ice dancing

Ice dancers perform to a variety of dance music, from the waltz to rock and roll. Separate movements and lifts are limited and throws are not allowed. All movements must be part of a dance sequence and skated to a dance rhythm.

In major ice-dancing competitions there are three parts. Compulsory dances count for 30 per cent of the total marks, set pattern 20 per cent and free dance 50 per cent.

▽ US ice dancers Elisa Spitz and Scott Gregory finish their free-dance routine with an elegant pose on the ice.

The free dance is the most popular and entertaining part of ice dancing. Ice dancers put a lot of work into planning their 4-minute program, and are always looking for new ideas or themes.

The judges award two sets of marks, for technical merit and for artistic impression.

△ World and Olympic champions in the early eighties, Jayne Torvill and Christopher Dean of Britain performing their Spanish theme. It earned them several sets of perfect marks, the maximum 6.0, in the set-pattern section.

Speed skating

Going all out on ice, some skaters have reached speeds of 50 km/h (30 mph) over short distances. In the longer races, skaters travel nearly twice as fast as runners.

▽ Speed skaters adopt a low, crouching position and take long, smooth strides. They use their arms for balance as they go around the curves.

Speed skaters race on a standard 400 m (436 yd) track with two lanes. In major competitions, only two racers take part at the same time, changing lanes once every lap. The placings are decided on times, after everyone has skated.

Races are held over distances from the 500 m (547 yd) sprint to 10,000 m (6.2 miles).

△ Speed skaters race two at a time in separate lanes. They wear body-hugging cat-suits and headgear to cut down wind resistance.

Ice hockey

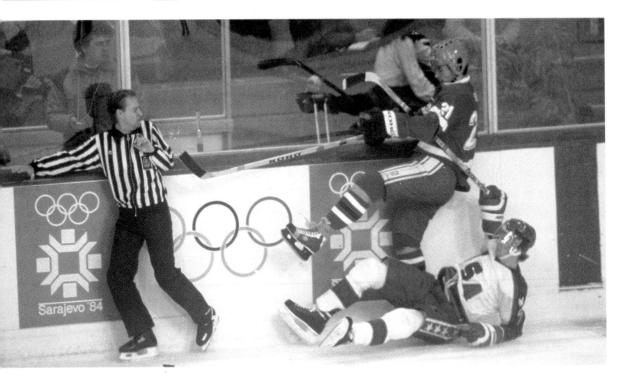

Ice hockey is played six to a side, with three forwards (right wing, center, left wing), two defenders (right and left) and a goalkeeper. Up to 14 substitutes are allowed.

Substitutions may be made at any time, provided a team does not have more than six players on the ice.

A match consists of three 20-minute periods of actual play. The clock is stopped whenever play stops.

△ Ice hockey is a fast game. The players, who constantly crash into each other or the boards, wear helmets and plenty of padding. There are many substitutions. Outfield players are rarely on the ice for more than five playing minutes at a time.

▷ The goalie, unless injured, usually plays the whole match. He has extra protection because a hard puck can be dangerous.

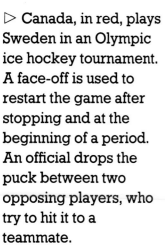
▷ Canada, in red, plays
Sweden in an Olympic
ice hockey tournament.
A face-off is used to
restart the game after
stopping and at the
beginning of a period.
An official drops the
puck between two
opposing players, who
try to hit it to a
teammate.

Face-offs take place
at the nearest face-off
spot to where the stop
occurred, or in the
center circle at the start
of a period. Only the
two players facing off
are allowed within the
face-off circles or
closer than 4.5 m (5 yd)
to the face-off spot.

Matches are refereed by officials on the ice, with the help of timekeepers and goal judges.

Players who break the rules serve time penalties in the penalty box. Penalties vary from 2 minutes actual playing time for minor offenses to 5 or 10 minutes for major ones. In extreme cases, a player may be sent off for the rest of the match. Players in the penalty box may not be substituted.

△ With players coming into physical contact at high speed, tempers often flare in ice hockey and fights sometimes break out. Players who commit offenses are sent to the penalty box. While a player serves his penalty, his team plays without him. Two-minute penalties are given for offenses such as tripping or elbowing, 5 minutes for fighting, and 10 minutes for serious misconduct or abusive language.

The puck may be passed between team mates in the same zone, but a player is offside if he moves into the attacking zone ahead of the puck.

Players may stop the puck in the air with an open hand, but only the goalies are allowed to catch it. Players may use their hands or feet to slide the puck along the ice but not to pass it or score in this way.

A team in their defending zone may take the puck behind their goal only once before advancing with it.

▽ A forward takes the puck around the back of the goal in an attempt to maneuver the opposing defense out of position. As well as being fast, ice hockey is a very tactical game. It has its individual stars, but good teamwork is what wins matches.

Other ice sports

△ Ice racing is popular in the United States, the Soviet Union and Sweden. It is like a speedway on ice.

◁ The bikes have special tires, with spikes to grip the smooth surface of the track.

◁ In curling, players take turns to slide disc-shaped "stones" toward a target, the "tee." Curlers use special brooms to sweep the ice in front of a teammate's stone to change its speed and direction. A team scores a point for each stone nearer to the tee than their opponents' nearest stone.

▽ Ice boating takes place on frozen lakes and seas. The boats move on sharp-edged runners.

The story of ice sports

The first skates

The first skates were made over 2,000 years ago from the bones of animals such as reindeer. These early skates were used by people as a means of transportation, to move about more easily on waterways that were iced up. It was the most convenient way for traders and other people to go about their business in freezing weather.

△ Dancing and skating on a frozen lake near Paris over 120 years ago.

△ Skating to market on a Dutch canal in olden times. The long skates are strapped onto the skaters' shoes.

Skating as a pastime

Skating for pleasure goes back a few hundred years, to the Netherlands. The British took it up, and the world's first ice club was formed in Edinburgh in 1742. The activity spread to France and Germany.

The sport develops

The British began to develop skating as a sport in the 1840s. It was soon introduced into the United States and Canada by British servicemen.

It was an American, Jackson Haines of Chicago, who developed the first spectacular skating techniques. Originally a ballroom dancer, he won a skating championship before going to Europe, where he founded the Viennese school of skating.

Although people raced on ice

△ A skating race in the early 1900s.

before figure skating developed as a sport, speed skating did not become organized until the National Skating Association of Great Britain was formed in 1879. But it was in the Scandinavian countries that this sport first became popular.

Ice hockey probably originated in Ontario, Canada, where in 1860 some Englishmen played a game on ice, using a type of puck. It developed as a Canadian sport, and rules were drawn up by students of McGill University in Montreal, about 20 years later.

△ A team of ladies at practice in Canada where ice hockey originated.

Championships

Men's world championships were first held in 1893 for speed skating and 1896 for figure skating, which also featured in the 1908 Olympics, in London. Ice hockey was introduced as an Olympic sport in 1920.

The first separate Winter

△ Canada (the winner) plays the United States in the 1932 Olympic tournament at Lake Placid, New York. Players wore very little protective equipment in those days.

Olympics were held at Chamonix, France, in 1924, when men's speed skating was added to the Olympic ice sports.

The last ice sport to win worldwide popularity was ice dancing, which became an Olympic sport in 1976.

Indoor ice rinks

The first mechanically refrigerated ice rink was probably a small private one called the Glaciarium, built in London, in 1876. But it was not until the 1930s, when new freezing methods were developed, that indoor rinks began to be built in great numbers. Now skaters everywhere can enjoy skating the whole year round.

Facts and records

The first ice star

Norwegian figure skater Sonja Henie won a record 10 consecutive world titles (1927–36) and 3 Olympic gold medals (1928–36). As a professional, she later made films in Hollywood featuring her grace, beauty and skills on ice, helping to popularize the sport around the world.

Fastest means of transport

The world record for iceboating was set in 1938 by US sailor John Buckstaff. He reached a speed of 230 km/h (143 mph).

In the early 1600s; iceboats traveling at about 80 km/h (50 mph) were the world's fastest means of transport.

Golden boy

US speed skater Eric Heiden won all five titles, from 500 m to 10,000 m, in the 1980 Winter Olympics, at Lake Placid. He is the only competitor to win five individual gold medals at one Olympic Games, summer or winter, in any sport.

◁ Sonja Henie. △ Speed skating star Eric Heiden.

Glossary

Curling
A game played by sliding large, heavy stones across the ice.

Face-off
A way of starting and restarting the game in ice hockey. An official drops the puck between the sticks of two opposing players.

Figures
Shapes traced on the ice with the skates as a section of figure-skating competition.

Figure skating
The branch of skating in which skaters perform artistic and athletic movements on the ice.

Free skating
The section of figure skating in which the competitors skate their own program.

Goal judges
The officials in ice hockey – one at each end of the rink – who determine whether the puck has crossed the line between the goalposts to score a goal.

Ice dancing
The sport in which partners skate to dance rhythms.

Ice racing
A type of speedway on ice, with riders racing around an oval track on machines with spiked wheels.

Lift
A movement in pair skating in which the male lifts his partner off the ice.

Offside
An illegal move in ice hockey when a player moves into his attacking zone before the puck.

Puck
The hard, rubber disc used in ice hockey instead of a ball.

Speed skating
Racing on ice skates.

Stones
The objects that curlers slide across the ice to a target.

Tee
The target in curling.

Zones
Divisions of an ice hockey rink.

Index